EQUAL OPPORTUNITIES COMMISSION

CODE OF PRACTICE

EQUAL OPPORTUNITY POLICIES,
PROCEDURES AND PRACTICES
IN EMPLOYMENT

LONDON: HER MAJESTY'S STATIONERY OFFICE

© Crown copyright 1985
First published 1985

ISBN 011 701279 3

Contents

CODE OF PRACTICE

The Equal Opportunities Commission (the EOC) was set up under the Sex Discrimination Act 1975 (as amended) and is empowered to issue Codes of Practice under section 56(A)(1) of that Act.

A failure on the part of any person to observe any provision of a code of practice shall not of itself render him [or her] liable to any proceedings; but in any proceedings under this Act before an industrial tribunal any code of practice issued under this section shall be admissible in evidence, and if any provision of such a code appears to the tribunal to be relevant to any question arising in the proceedings it shall be taken into account in determining that question.

[*Sex Discrimination Act 1975 (as amended), section 56A(10)*]

INTRODUCTION

1. The EOC issues this Code of Practice for the following purposes:

   (a) for the elimination of discrimination in employment

   (b) to give guidance as to what steps it is reasonably practicable for employers to take to ensure that their employees do not in the course of their employment act unlawfully contrary to the Sex Discrimination Act (SDA)

   (c) for the promotion of equality of opportunity between men and women in employment.

   The SDA prohibits discrimination against men, as well as against women. It also requires that married people should not be treated less favourably than single people of the same sex.

   It should be noted that the provisions of the SDA – and therefore of this Code – apply to the UK-based subsidiaries of foreign companies.

2. The Code gives guidance to employers, trade unions and employment agencies on measures which can be taken to achieve equality. The chances of success of any organisation will clearly be improved if it seeks to develop the abilities of all employees, and the Code shows the close link which exists between equal opportunity and good employment practice. In some cases, an initial cost may be involved, but this should be more than compensated for by better relationships and better use of human resources.

SMALL BUSINESSES

3. The Code has to deal in general terms and it will be necessary for employers to adapt it in a way appropriate to the size and structure of their organisations. Small businesses, for example, will require much simpler procedures than organisations with complex structures and it may not always be reasonable for them to carry out all the Code's detailed recommendations. In adapting the Code's recommendations, small firms should, however, ensure that their practices comply with the Sex Discrimination Act.

EMPLOYERS' RESPONSIBILITY

4. **The primary responsibility at law rests with each employer to ensure that there is no unlawful discrimination.** It is important, however, that measures to eliminate discrimination or promote equality of opportunity should be understood and supported by all employees. Employers are therefore recommended to involve their employees in equal opportunity policies.

INDIVIDUAL EMPLOYEES' RESPONSIBILITY

5. While the main responsibility for eliminating discrimination and providing equal opportunity is that of the employer, individual employees at all levels have responsibilities too. They must not discriminate or knowingly aid their employer to do so.

TRADE UNION RESPONSIBILITY

6. The full commitment of trade unions is essential for the elimination of discrimination and for the successful operation of an equal opportunities policy. Much can be achieved by collective bargaining and throughout the Code it is assumed that all the normal procedures will be followed.

7. It is recommended that unions should co-operate in the introduction and implementation of equal opportunities policies where employers have decided to introduce them, and should urge that such policies be adopted where they have not yet been introduced.

8. Trade Unions have a responsibility to ensure that their representatives and members do not unlawfully discriminate on grounds of sex or marriage in the admission or treatment of members. The guidance in this Code also applies to trade unions in their role as employers.

EMPLOYMENT AGENCIES

9. Employment agencies have a responsibility as suppliers of job applicants to avoid unlawful discrimination on the grounds of sex or marriage in providing services to clients. The guidance in this Code also applies to employment agencies in their role as employers.

DEFINITIONS

10. For ease of reference, the main employment provisions of the Sex Discrimination Act, including definitions of direct and indirect sex and marriage discrimination, are provided in a Legal Annex to this Code. (See pages 17-23).

PART 1

THE ROLE OF GOOD EMPLOYMENT PRACTICES IN ELIMINATING SEX AND MARRIAGE DISCRIMINATION

11. This section of the Code describes those good employment practices which will help to eliminate unlawful discrimination. It recommends the establishment and use of consistent criteria for selection, training, promotion, redundancy and dismissal which are made known to all employees. Without this consistency, decisions can be subjective and leave the way open for unlawful discrimination to occur.

RECRUITMENT

12. It is unlawful: UNLESS THE JOB IS COVERED BY AN EXCEPTION:*
TO DISCRIMINATE DIRECTLY OR INDIRECTLY ON THE GROUNDS OF SEX OR MARRIAGE

  - IN THE ARRANGEMENTS MADE FOR DECIDING WHO SHOULD BE OFFERED A JOB

  - IN ANY TERMS OF EMPLOYMENT

  - BY REFUSING OR OMITTING TO OFFER A PERSON EMPLOYMENT

  [*Section 6(1)(a); 6(1)(b); 6(1)(c)*]†

13. It is therefore recommended that:

  (a) each individual should be assessed according to his or her personal capability to carry out a given job. It should not be assumed that men only or women only will be able to perform certain kinds of work;

  (b) any qualifications or requirements applied to a job which effectively inhibit applications from one sex or from married people should be retained only if they are justifiable in terms of the job to be done;

  [*Section 6(1)(a), together with section 1(1)(b) or 3(1)(b)*]

  (c) any age limits should be retained only if they are necessary for the job. An unjustifiable age limit could constitute unlawful indirect discrimination, for example, against women who have taken time out of employment for child-rearing;

  (d) where trade unions uphold such qualifications or requirements as union policy, they should amend that policy in the light of any potentially unlawful effect.

GENUINE OCCUPATIONAL QUALIFICATIONS (GOQs)

14. It is unlawful: EXCEPT FOR CERTAIN JOBS WHEN A PERSON'S SEX IS A GENUINE OCCUPATIONAL QUALIFICATION (GOQ) FOR THAT JOB to select candidates on the ground of sex.

  [*Section 7(2); 7(3) and 7(4)*]

---

* There are a number of exceptions to the requirements of the SDA, that employers must not discriminate against their employees or against potential employees. The main exceptions are mentioned on pages 17/18 of the Legal Annex.
† For the full text of section 6 or other sections of the Sex Discrimination Act referred to in this Code, readers are advised to consult a copy of the Act which is available from Her Majesty's Stationery Office.

15. There are very few instances in which a job will qualify for a GOQ on the ground of sex. However, exceptions may arise*, for example, where considerations of privacy and decency or authenticity are involved. The SDA expressly states that the need of the job for strength and stamina does not justify restricting it to men. When a GOQ exists for a job, it applies also to promotion, transfer, or training for that job, but cannot be used to justify a dismissal.

16. In some instances, the GOQ will apply to some of the duties only. A GOQ will not be valid, however, where members of the appropriate sex are already employed in sufficient numbers to meet the employer's likely requirements without undue inconvenience. For example, in a job where sales assistants may be required to undertake changing room duties, it might not be lawful to claim a GOQ in respect of *all* the assistants on the grounds that any of them might be required to undertake changing room duties from time to time.

17. It is therefore recommended that:

   - A job for which a GOQ was used in the past should be re-examined if the post falls vacant to see whether the GOQ still applies. Circumstances may well have changed, rendering the GOQ inapplicable.

SOURCES OF RECRUITMENT

18. It is unlawful: UNLESS THE JOB IS COVERED BY AN EXCEPTION:

   - TO DISCRIMINATE ON GROUNDS OF SEX OR MARRIAGE IN THE ARRANGEMENTS MADE FOR DETERMINING WHO SHOULD BE OFFERED EMPLOYMENT WHETHER RECRUITING BY ADVERTISE-MENTS, THROUGH EMPLOYMENT AGENCIES, JOBCENTRES, OR CAREER OFFICES.

   - TO IMPLY THAT APPLICATIONS FROM ONE SEX OR FROM MARRIED PEOPLE WILL NOT BE CONSIDERED.

   [*Section 6(1)(a))*]

   - TO INSTRUCT OR PUT PRESSURE ON OTHERS TO OMIT TO REFER FOR EMPLOYMENT PEOPLE OF ONE SEX OR MARRIED PEOPLE UNLESS THE JOB IS COVERED BY AN EXCEPTION.

   [*Sections 39 and 40*]

   It is also unlawful WHEN ADVERTISING JOB VACANCIES,

   - TO PUBLISH OR CAUSE TO BE PUBLISHED AN ADVERTISEMENT WHICH INDICATES OR MIGHT REASONABLY BE UNDERSTOOD AS INDICATING AN INTENTION TO DISCRIMINATE UNLAWFULLY ON GROUNDS OF SEX OR MARRIAGE.

   [*Section 38*]

---

* See page 18 of Legal Annex

19. It is therefore recommended that:

Advertising

(a) job advertising should be carried out in such a way as to encourage applications from suitable candidates of both sexes. This can be achieved both by wording of the advertisements and, for example, by placing advertisements in publications likely to reach both sexes. All advertising material and accompanying literature relating to employment or training issues should be reviewed to ensure that it avoids presenting men and women in stereotyped roles. Such stereotyping tends to perpetuate sex segregation in jobs and can also lead people of the opposite sex to believe that they would be unsuccessful in applying for particular jobs;

(b) where vacancies are filled by promotion or transfer, they should be published to all eligible employees in such a way that they do not restrict applications from either sex;

(c) recruitment solely or primarily by word of mouth may unnecessarily restrict the choice of applicants available. The method should be avoided in a workforce predominantly of one sex, if in practice it prevents members of the opposite sex from applying;

(d) where applicants are supplied through trade unions and members of one sex only come forward, this should be discussed with the unions and an alternative approach adopted.

Careers Service/Schools

20. When notifying vacancies to the Careers Service, employers should specify that these are open to both boys and girls. This is especially important when a job has traditionally been done exclusively or mainly by one sex. If dealing with single sex schools, they should ensure, where possible, that both boys' and girls' schools are approached; it is also a good idea to remind mixed schools that jobs are open to boys and girls.

SELECTION METHODS

Tests

21. (a) If selection tests are used, they should be specifically related to job and/or career requirements and should measure an individual's actual or inherent ability to do or train for the work or career.

(b) Tests should be reviewed regularly to ensure that they remain relevant and free from any unjustifiable bias, either in content or in scoring mechanism.

Applications and Interviewing

22. It is unlawful: UNLESS THE JOB IS COVERED BY AN EXCEPTION:

TO DISCRIMINATE ON GROUNDS OF SEX OR MARRIAGE BY REFUSING OR DELIBERATELY OMITTING TO OFFER EMPLOYMENT.

[Section 6(1)(c)]

23. It is therefore recommended that:

    (a) employers should ensure that personnel staff, line managers and all other employees who may come into contact with job applicants, should be trained in the provisions of the SDA, including the fact that it is unlawful to instruct or put pressure on others to discriminate;

    (b) applications from men and women should be processed in exactly the same way. For example, there should not be separate lists of male and female or married and single applicants. All those handling applications and conducting interviews should be trained in the avoidance of unlawful discrimination and records of interviews kept, where practicable, showing why applicants were or were not appointed;

    (c) questions should relate to the requirements of the job. Where it is necessary to assess whether personal circumstances will affect performance of the job (for example, where it involves unsocial hours or extensive travel) this should be discussed objectively without detailed questions based on assumptions about marital status, children and domestic obligations. Questions about marriage plans or family intentions should not be asked, as they could be construed as showing bias against women. Information necessary for personnel records can be collected after a job offer has been made.

PROMOTION, TRANSFER AND TRAINING

24. It is unlawful: UNLESS THE JOB IS COVERED BY AN EXCEPTION, FOR EMPLOYERS TO DISCRIMINATE DIRECTLY OR INDIRECTLY ON THE GROUNDS OF SEX OR MARRIAGE IN THE WAY THEY AFFORD ACCESS TO OPPORTUNITIES FOR PROMOTION, TRANSFER OR TRAINING.

[*Section 6(2)(a)*]

25. It is therefore recommended that:

    (a) where an appraisal system in in operation, the assessment criteria should be examined to ensure that they are not unlawfully discriminatory and the scheme monitored to assess how it is working in practice;

    (b) when a group of workers predominantly of one sex is excluded from an appraisal scheme, access to promotion, transfer and training and to other benefits should be reviewed, to ensure that there is no unlawful indirect discrimination;

    (c) promotion and career development patterns are reviewed to ensure that the traditional qualifications are justifiable requirements for the job to be done. In some circumstances, for example, promotion on the basis of length of service could amount to unlawful indirect discrimination, as it may unjustifiably affect more women than men;

    (d) when general ability and personal qualities are the main requirements for promotion to a post, care should be taken to consider favourably candidates of both sexes with differing career patterns and general experience;

    (e) rules which restrict or preclude transfer between certain jobs should be questioned and changed if they are found to be unlawfully discriminatory. Employees of one sex may be concentrated in sections from which transfers are traditionally restricted without real justification;

(f) policies and practices regarding selection for training, day release and personal development should be examined for unlawful direct and indirect discrimination. Where there is found to be an imbalance in training as between sexes, the cause should be identified to ensure that it is not discriminatory;

(g) age limits for access to training and promotion should be questioned.

HEALTH AND SAFETY LEGISLATION

26. Equal treatment of men and women may be limited by statutory provisions which require men and women to be treated differently. For example, the Factories Act 1961 places restrictions on the hours of work of female manual employees, although the Health and Safety Executive can exempt employers from these restrictions, subject to certain conditions. The Mines and Quarries Act 1954 imposes limitations on women's work and there are restrictions where there is special concern for the unborn child (e.g. lead and ionising radiation). However the broad duties placed on employers by the Health and Safety at Work, etc., Act, 1974 makes no distinctions between men and women. Section 2(1) requires employers to ensure, so far as is reasonably practicable, the health and safety and welfare at work of *all* employees.

SPECIFIC HEALTH AND SAFETY REQUIREMENTS UNDER EARLIER LEGISLATION ARE UNAFFECTED BY THE ACT.

It is therefore recommended that

– company policy should be reviewed and serious consideration given to any significant differences in treatment between men and women, and there should be well-founded reasons if such differences are maintained or introduced.

TERMS OF EMPLOYMENT, BENEFITS, FACILITIES AND SERVICES

27. It is unlawful: UNLESS THE JOB IS COVERED BY AN EXCEPTION:

TO DISCRIMINATE ON THE GROUNDS OF SEX OR MARRIAGE, DIRECTLY OR INDIRECTLY, IN THE TERMS ON WHICH EMPLOYMENT IS OFFERED OR IN AFFORDING ACCESS TO ANY BENEFITS*, FACILITIES OR SERVICES

[*Sections 6(1)(b); 6(2)(a); 29*]

28. It is therefore recommended that:

(a) all terms of employment, benefits, facilities and services are reviewed to ensure that there is no unlawful discrimination on grounds of sex or marriage. For example, part-time work, domestic leave, company cars and benefits for dependants should be available to both male and female employees in the same or not materially different circumstances.

29. In an establishment where part-timers are solely or mainly women, unlawful indirect discrimination may arise if, as a group, they are treated less favourably than other employees without justification.

It is therefore recommended that:

(b) where part-time workers do not enjoy pro-rata pay or benefits with full-time workers, the arrangements should be reviewed to ensure that they are justified without regard to sex.

---

* Certain provisions relating to death and retirement are exempt from the Act.

GRIEVANCES, DISCIPLINARY PROCEDURES AND VICTIMISATION

30. It is unlawful: TO VICTIMISE AN INDIVIDUAL FOR A COMPLAINT MADE IN GOOD FAITH ABOUT SEX OR MARRIAGE DISCRIMINATION OR FOR GIVING EVIDENCE ABOUT SUCH A COMPLAINT.

    [Section 4(1); 4(2); and 4(3)]

31. It is therefore recommended that:

    (a) particular care is taken to ensure that an employee who has in good faith taken action under the Sex Discrimination Act or the Equal Pay Act does not receive less favourable treatment than other employees, for example by being disciplined or dismissed;

    (b) employees should be advised to use the internal procedures, where appropriate, but this is without prejudice to the individual's right to apply to an industrial tribunal within the statutory time limit, i.e. before the end of the period of three months beginning when the act complained of was done. (There is no time limit if the victimisation is continuing.);

    (c) particular care is taken to deal effectively with all complaints of discrimination, victimisation or harassment. It should not be assumed that they are made by those who are over-sensitive.

DISMISSALS, REDUNDANCIES AND OTHER UNFAVOURABLE TREATMENT OF EMPLOYEES

32. It is unlawful: TO DISCRIMINATE DIRECTLY OR INDIRECTLY ON GROUNDS OF SEX OR MARRIAGE IN DISMISSALS OR BY TREATING AN EMPLOYEE UNFAVOURABLY IN ANY OTHER WAY.

    [Section 6(2)(b)]

    It is therefore recommended that:

    (a) care is taken that members of one sex are not disciplined or dismissed for performance or behaviour which would be overlooked or condoned in the other sex;

    (b) redundancy procedures affecting a group of employees predominantly of one sex should be reviewed, so as to remove any effects which could be disproportionate and unjustifiable;

    (c) conditions of access to voluntary redundancy benefit* should be made available on equal terms to male and female employees in the same or not materially different circumstances;

    (d) where there is down-grading or short-time working (for example, owing to a change in the nature or volume of an employer's business) the arrangements should not unlawfully discriminate on the ground of sex;

    (e) all reasonably practical steps should be taken to ensure that a standard of conduct or behaviour is observed which prevents members of either sex from being intimidated, harassed or otherwise subjected to unfavourable treatment on the ground of their sex.

---

* Certain provisions relating to death and retirement are exempt from the Act.

PART 2

THE ROLE OF GOOD EMPLOYMENT PRACTICES IN PROMOTING EQUALITY OF OPPORTUNITY

33. This section of the Code describes those employment practices which help to promote equality of opportunity. It gives information about the formulation and implementation of equal opportunities policies. While such policies are not required by law, their value has been recognised by a number of employers who have voluntarily adopted them. Others may wish to follow this example.

FORMULATING AN EQUAL OPPORTUNITIES POLICY

34. An equal opportunities policy will ensure the effective use of human resources in the best interests of both the organisation and its employees. It is a commitment by an employer to the development and use of employment procedures and practices which do not discriminate on grounds of sex or marriage and which provide genuine equality of opportunity for all employees. The detail of the policy will vary according to size of the organisation.

IMPLEMENTING THE POLICY

35. An equal opportunities policy must be seen to have the active support of management at the highest level. To ensure that the policy is fully effective, the following procedure is recommended:

    (a) the policy should be clearly stated and, where appropriate, included in a collective agreement;

    (b) overall responsibility for implementing the policy should rest with senior management;

    (c) the policy should be made known to all employees and, where reasonably practicable, to all job applicants.

36. Trade unions have a very important part to play in implementing genuine equality of opportunity and they will obviously be involved in the review of established procedures to ensure that these are consistent with the law.

MONITORING

37. It is recommended that the policy is monitored regularly to ensure that it is working in practice. Consideration could be given to setting up a joint Management/Trade Union Review Committee.

38. In a small firm with a simple structure it may be quite adequate to assess the distribution and payment of employees from personal knowledge.

39. In a large and complex organisation a more formal analysis will be necessary, for example, by sex, grade and payment in each unit. This may need to be introduced by stages as resources permit. Any formal analysis should be regularly updated and available to Management and Trade Unions to enable any necessary action to be taken.

40. Sensible monitoring will show, for example, whether members of one sex:

    (a) do not apply for employment or promotion, or that fewer apply than might be expected;

(b) are not recruited, promoted or selected for training and development or are appointed/selected in a significantly lower proportion than their rate of application;

(c) are concentrated in certain jobs, sections or departments.

POSITIVE ACTION

Recruitment, Training and Promotion

41. Selection for recruitment or promotion must be on merit, irrespective of sex. However, the Sex Discrimination Act does allow certain steps to redress the effects of previous unequal opportunities. Where there have been few or no members of one sex in particular work in their employment for the previous 12 months, the Act allows employers to give special encouragement to, and provide specific training for, the minority sex. Such measures are usually described as Positive Action.

[*Section 48*]

42. Employers may wish to consider positive measures such as:

(a) training their own employees (male or female) for work which is traditionally the preserve of the other sex, for example, training women for skilled manual or technical work;

(b) positive encouragement to women to apply for management posts – special courses may be needed;

(c) advertisements which encourage applications from the minority sex, but make it clear that selection will be on merit without reference to sex;

(d) notifying job agencies, as part of a Positive Action Programme that they wish to encourage members of one sex to apply for vacancies, where few or no members of that sex are doing the work in question. In these circumstances, job agencies should tell both men and women about the posts and, in addition, let the under-represented sex know that applications from them are particularly welcome. Withholding information from one sex in an attempt to encourage applications from the opposite sex would be unlawful.

Other Working Arrangements

43. There are other forms of action which could assist both employer and employee by helping to provide continuity of employment to working parents, many of whom will have valuable experience or skills.

Employers may wish to consider with their employees whether:

(a) certain jobs can be carried out on a part-time or flexi-time basis;

(b) personal leave arrangements are adequate and available to both sexes. It should not be assumed that men may not need to undertake domestic responsibilities on occasion, especially at the time of childbirth;

(c) child-care facilities are available locally or whether it would be feasible to establish nursery facilities on the premises or combine with other employers to provide them;

(d) residential training could be facilitated for employees with young children. For example, where this type of training is necessary, by informing staff who are selected well in advance to enable them to make childcare and other personal arrangements; employers with their own residential training centres could also consider whether childcare facilities might be provided;

(e) the statutory maternity leave provisions could be enhanced, for example, by reducing the qualifying service period, extending the leave period, or giving access to part-time arrangements on return.

These arrangements, and others, are helpful to both sexes but are of particular benefit to women in helping them to remain in gainful employment during the years of child-rearing.

ANNEX

LEGAL BACKGROUND

This section gives general guidance only and should not be regarded as a complete or definitive statement of law.

THE RELATIONSHIP BETWEEN THE EQUAL PAY ACT AND THE SEX DISCRIMINATION ACT

The Sex Discrimination Act 1975 (as amended) (the SDA) covers a wide range of non-contractual benefits, in addition to covering practices and procedures relating to recruitment, training, promotion and dismissal. A claim relating to a contractual benefit may also be brought under the SDA provided the benefit does not consist of the payment of money.

The Equal Pay Act 1970 (as amended) (the EPA) provides for an individual to be treated not less favourably than a person of the opposite sex who works for the same employer, as regards **pay and other terms of the contract of employment** where they are employed on like work (i.e. the same work or work which is broadly similar) or on work which has been rated as equivalent under a job evaluation scheme or on work which is of equal value.

There is no overlap between an individual's rights under the Equal Pay Act and those under the Sex Discrimination Act. All complaints of discrimination in the circumstances covered by the EPA are dealt with under that Act. All complaints of discrimination about access to jobs and matters not included in a contract of employment and about contractual matters (other than those relating to the payment of money) in situations not covered by the EPA are dealt with under the SDA.

WHO IS COVERED BY THE SDA?

The provisions of the SDA apply to both men and women. It is unlawful to discriminate, directly or indirectly, against a person on the grounds of sex or marriage, unless the situation is covered by one of the Exceptions. It is also unlawful to instruct or bring pressure to bear on others to discriminate.

EXCEPTIONS FROM THE ACT

Geographical Scope
Section 10(1)

The SDA does not relate to employment which is wholly or mainly outside Great Britain.

Private Household or Small Employer
Section 6(3)(a); Section 6(3)(b)

These exceptions make it lawful under the Sex Discrimination Act to discriminate in relation to existing or potential employment in a private household, or an organisation which employs five people or fewer.* These exceptions do not apply to matters covered by the Equal Pay Act.

Discrimination ("victimisation") under section 4 of the SDA is not excluded by these exceptions.

---

* However in the light of a judgement of the European Court of Justice in Luxembourg (165/82 of 8th November 1983), these exceptions will be subject to amendment in the near future.

Death or Retirement
Section 6(4)

Certain provisions relating to death or retirement are exempt from the SDA.

Pregnancy or Childbirth
Section 2(2)

Special treatment (i.e. more favourable treatment) may lawfully be afforded to women in connection with pregnancy or childbirth.

Genuine Occupational Qualifications
Section 7

A person's sex may be a Genuine Occupational Qualification (GOQ) for a job, in which case discrimination in recruitment, opportunities for promotion or transfer to, or training for such employment would not be unlawful. A GOQ cannot, however, apply to the treatment of employees once they are in post, nor to discrimination on grounds of marriage, nor to victimisation.

The GOQ is not an automatic exception for general categories of jobs. In every case it will be necessary for an employer to show that the criteria detailed in the SDA apply to the job or part of the job in question.

A GOQ may be claimed only because of:

(a) physiology (excluding physical strength and stamina) or authenticity – for example, a model or an actor.

(b) decency or privacy – for example, some changing room attendants.

(c) the nature or location of the establishment which makes it impracticable for the jobholder to live in premises other than those provided by the employer (e.g. if the job is in a ship or on a remote site) and the only available premises for persons doing that kind of job do not provide both separate sleeping accommodation for each sex, and sanitary facilities which can be used in privacy from the other. In such a case, the employer may discriminate by choosing for the job only persons of the same sex as those who are already living, or normally live, in these premises. However, the exception does not apply if the employer could reasonably be expected either to equip the premises with the necessary separate sleeping accommodation and private sanitary facilities, or to provide other premises, for a jobholder of the opposite sex.

(d) the fact that the establishment, or part of it, provides special care, supervision or attention to people of one sex only – for example, some jobs in a single-sex hospital.

(e) the fact that the job involves the provision of personal services, promoting welfare or education, that are most effectively provided by men (or by women) – for example, some probation officers or wardens of residential hostels.

(f) laws regulating the employment of women.

(g) the laws and customs of the country in which part of the job is to be carried out – for example, a job involving driving in a country where women are forbidden to drive.

(h) the fact that the job is one of two to be held by a married couple.

DEFINITION OF "EMPLOYMENT"
Section 82

"Employment" is defined in the SDA as meaning employment under a contract of service or of apprenticeship or a contract personally to carry out any work or labour.

DIRECT SEX DISCRIMINATION
Section 1(1)(a)

This occurs where a person of one sex is treated less favourably, on the ground of sex, than a person of the other sex would be in the same or not materially different circumstances.

INDIRECT SEX DISCRIMINATION
Section 1(1)(b)

Indirect sex discrimination occurs when an unjustifiable requirement or condition is applied equally to both sexes, but has a disproportionately adverse effect on one sex, because the proportion of one sex which can comply with it is much smaller than the proportion of the other sex which can comply with it. For example, a requirement to be mobile might bar more women than men. A complainant would have to show that fewer women than men could comply with such a requirement and that it is to her detriment that she cannot comply. Where the employer can justify such a requirement without regard to sex there will be no unlawful act. A finding of unlawful discrimination may be made even though the employer has no intention to discriminate.

MARRIAGE DISCRIMINATION
Section 3(1)(a); Section 3(1)(b)

Direct discrimination against a married person occurs where a married person is treated less favourably on the grounds of marital status, than an unmarried person of the same sex would be in the same or not materially different circumstances. Indirect discrimination against a married person is similar in concept to indirect sex discrimination and may arise when a condition or requirement is applied equally to married and unmarried persons of the same sex but which is in fact discriminatory in its effect on married persons. For example, a requirement to be mobile might bar more married than single women.

DISCRIMINATION BY WAY OF VICTIMISATION
Section 4

This occurs where a person is treated less favourably than other persons would be treated because he/she has done something by reference to the EPA or the SDA, for example, brought proceedings or given evidence or information in a case under either of those Acts or alleged (expressly or otherwise) that anyone has committed an act which could constitute a breach of those Acts. Victimisation is not unlawful if the allegation was false and not made in good faith.

DISCRIMINATION IN RECRUITMENT
Section 6(1)

This section makes it unlawful for an employer to discriminate when recruiting employees in the following ways:

Section 6(1)(a)

in the arrangements made for deciding who should be offered a job. (One example might be the instructions given to a Personnel Officer or to an Employment Agency. Another example might be advertising a job in a place where only one sex would have the opportunity of seeing the advertisement.)

Section 6(1)(b)

in relation to any terms offered (for instance, in respect of pay or holidays). It is, for instance, unlawful to offer a job (whether or not the candidate accepts), where the terms would be a breach of the EPA should an employment contract be entered into.

Section 6(1)(c)

by refusing or deliberately omitting to offer a person employment (for example, by rejecting an application or deliberately refusing consideration of an application).

DISCRIMINATION IN THE TREATMENT OF PRESENT EMPLOYEES
Section 6(2)

This section makes it unlawful for an employer to discriminate in the following ways:

Section 6(2)(a)

in the way access is afforded to opportunities for promotion, transfer or training, or to any other benefits*, facilities or services, or by refusing or deliberately omitting to afford access to them; or

Section 6(2)(b)

by dismissal or the subjection to any other unfavourable treatment.

Section 9
DISCRIMINATION AGAINST CONTRACT WORKERS

Section 9(1)

This section covers contract workers, i.e. workers who are sent to work for an organisation by another organisation which employs them.

Section 9(2)

It is unlawful for the principal firm to discriminate on grounds of sex or marriage:

(a) in the terms on which it allows the contract worker to do the work; or

(b) by not allowing the contract worker to do it or continue to do it; or

(c) in the way the contract worker is afforded access to any benefits, facilities or services or by refusing or deliberately omitting to afford access to any of them; or

(d) by subjecting the contract worker to any other unfavourable treatment.

Section 9(3)

A principal may rely upon the GOQ exception, where it is applicable, to refuse to allow a contract worker to do, or to continue to do the contract work.

---

* other than the payment of money provided under a contract of employment.

Section 9(4)

Where a principal provides his contract workers with benefits, facilities or services not materially different from those he provides to the public, a complaint relating to the discriminatory provision of such benefits, etc. would not fall under section 9, but under section 29 of the SDA.

DISCRIMINATION BY TRADE UNIONS AND EMPLOYERS' ORGANISATIONS, ETC.
Section 12(1) and 12(2)

It is unlawful, for an organisation of workers or of employers or any other organisation whose members carry on a particular profession or trade for the purposes of which the organisation exists, to discriminate on grounds of sex or marriage against anyone applying for membership:

(a) in the terms on which it is prepared to admit the person to membership; or

(b) by refusing or deliberately omitting to accept an application for membership.

Section 12(3)

It is unlawful for such an organisation to discriminate on grounds of sex or marriage against a member:

(a) in the way it affords access to any benefits, facilities or services or by refusing or deliberately omitting to afford access to them; or

(b) by depriving a person of membership or varying the terms of membership; or

(c) subjecting to any other unfavourable treatment.

DISCRIMINATION BY EMPLOYMENT AGENCIES
Section 15(1)

It is unlawful for an employment agency to discriminate on grounds of sex or marriage:

(a) in the terms on which they offer to provide any of their services; or

(b) by refusing or deliberately omitting to provide them; or

(c) in the way in which they provide any of them.

Section 15(4)

Section 15(1) will not apply if the discrimination only concerns employment which an employer could lawfully refuse to offer to a woman (or a man).

Section 15(5) and 15(6)

Where an employment agency has the employer's assurance that a vacancy is covered by one of the exceptions and this turns out not to be the case, the agency has a defence if it can prove both that it acted in reliance on a statement by the employer that its action would not be unlawful and that it was reasonable for it to rely on the statement. It is a summary offence punishable by a fine not exceeding £2,000, knowingly or recklessly to make such a statement which in a material respect is false or misleading.

Section 38
DISCRIMINATORY ADVERTISEMENTS

Section 38(1) and 38(2)

The SDA makes it unlawful to publish or cause to be published an advertisement which indicates, or might reasonably be taken to indicate, an intention to discriminate unlawfully. An advertisement would not be unlawful if it dealt with a job which was covered by an exception.

Section 38(3)

An advertisement which uses a job description with a sexual connotation (for example, 'waiter' 'salesgirl' or 'stewardess') is taken as an intention to commit an unlawful discriminatory act, unless the advertisement states that the job is open to men and women or uses descriptions applying to both sexes (e.g. 'waiter' or 'waitress').

Section 38(4)

There will be cases where a publisher may not know whether a particular advertisement is lawful. A publisher will not be held liable if:

(a) he or she relied on a statement by the person placing the advertisement that the publication would not be unlawful, for example because the vacancy was covered by an exception; and

(b) it was reasonable for the publisher to rely on the statement.

Section 38(5)

It is an offence punishable on summary conviction with a fine not exceeding £2,000, for anyone placing an advertisement knowingly or recklessly to make a materially false or misleading statement to the publisher as to its lawfulness.

INSTRUCTIONS TO DISCRIMINATE
Section 39

It is unlawful for a person who has authority over another person or whose wishes are normally carried out by that other person to instruct or attempt to procure another person (e.g. a member of staff) to carry out an act of unlawful discrimination, e.g. an instruction to an employment agency to discriminate.

PRESSURE TO DISCRIMINATE
Section 40

It is unlawful for a person to bring pressure to bear on another person to carry out an act of unlawful discrimination, by providing or offering any benefit or threatening any detriment; for example, by a threat of industrial action to persuade an employer to discriminate.

LIABILITY OF EMPLOYERS AND PRINCIPALS
Section 41

An employer is liable for any act done by an employee in the course of the employment with or without the employer's knowledge or approval, unless the employer can show that such steps were taken as were reasonably practicable to prevent the employee doing the act in question. Similarly, a principal is liable for any act done by an agent with the principal's authority.

Section 42

A person (for example, an employee or agent) who knowingly aids another to do an unlawful act is also to be treated as having done that act, unless it can be shown that he or she acted in reliance on a statement that the act would not be unlawful and that it was reasonable to rely on such a statement.

POSITIVE ACTION BY TRAINING BODIES
Section 47

Training bodies may apply to the Secretary of State for Employment to become designated for the purpose of providing:

(a) training or encouragement for particular work where in the previous 12 months one sex has been substantially under-represented, or

(b) special training for persons following absence from employment because of domestic or family responsibilities.

POSITIVE ACTION BY EMPLOYERS
Section 48

This section of the SDA allows for positive action by employers to overcome the effects of past discrimination. It allows for training and encouragement where few or no members of one sex have been doing particular work in the preceding 12 months. It does not cover recruitment or promotion.

Advice on the promotion of equality of opportunity in employment is available from the EOC. All EOC publications referred to are available from the EOC offices in Manchester, Glasgow and Cardiff:

Overseas House, Quay Street, Manchester M3 3HN

249 West George Street, Glasgow G2 4QE

Caerwys House, Windsor Lane, Cardiff CF1 1LB

EOC Publications

A Short Guide to the Sex Discrimination Act 1975

Equal Opportunities: A Guide for Employers

A Model Equal Opportunity Policy

The Sex Discrimination Act and Advertising

Fair Dealing – guidance notes on the Sex Discrimination Act for those in the Employment Services

Setting up a Workplace Nursery: A manual for employers and employees

Positive Sex Discrimination in Training Schemes: Guidance on how to apply for Designation under Section 47 of the Sex Discrimination Act 1975

Other Publications

Many Policy Statements will cover race as well as sex discrimination. For advice on racial discrimination refer to the Code of Practice issued by the Commission for Racial Equality.

Examples of equal opportunities policy statements are the Trade Union Congress Model Clause and the Confederation of British Industry's Statement Guide.

Printed in the UK FOR HMSO Dd 738255 C500 3/85